SLEDDING WITH THE SNOW DOGS

An Arctic Circle Adventure

Nina Olsson

Grosvenor House
Publishing Limited

This book is published by
Grosvenor House Publishing Ltd
Link House
140 The Broadway, Tolworth, Surrey, KT6 7HT.
www.grosvenorhousepublishing.co.uk

A CIP record for this book
is available from the British Library

ISBN 978-1-78623-361-5

This book is dedicated to all those who have braved the Arctic snows, especially Collette who looked after me in the cold beautiful landscape. And to five wonderful Huskies who showed this amateur what to do.

Contents

PHOTOGRAPHIC PLATES

*   Photographs by Collette Chapman
* *   'Sled Train' by Mike Turner
* * * Taken by Restaurant Staff

All other photographs by Nina Olsson

Photographs printed by Photo Corner Ltd, previously Fairs Cameras, Bebington Wirral.

Cover Artwork by David Bixter

Preface

2007

"That looks interesting." A phrase that at various times in my life, has set me off on all sorts of adventures. On this occasion, it resulted in being on the end of a sled pulled by five huskies, through stunning Arctic terrain.

How did that come to be?

I had gone to my local veterinary practice with one of my cats, and while in the queue to pay, my eyes strayed around the room and alighted on a poster. 'Come to the Arctic' it said, 'and take part in a Charity Challenge Run, Dog teams, open air etc., etc.' Now, I thought, that looks...

Once home, I phoned for further details and, buoyed up with rash enthusiasm, I heard myself agreeing to take part in the adventure. The information pack duly arrived and still being of the same, if not quite sound, mind, I signed up.

The experience was to take place in the April of the following year, thus allowing time to raise the required funds. I mentioned it to my friend Collette, who immediately signed up.

I had always been enthralled by stories about polar expeditions, especially about Scott and Amundsen (not that this was anything like those, not even the same Pole), however, this was my polar, well nearly polar, well many miles away polar, expedition. Intrepid explorer Olsson, it sounded good. Well, we all have our dreams don't we, and this would be the nearest I would ever get to anything like that.

I had, some years earlier, purchased some old picture frames, and behind the painting in one of them was an old photograph of a husky team and their musher.

It had been taken in 1954 of an expedition to the Larsen A ice shelf, on the Nordenskjold coast. I was fascinated and consequently did further research.

I wrote to the British Antarctic Survey (known as the Falkland Islands Dependency Survey then) and received back interesting information about my photograph. I had been looking at Bill and the Gangsters, who were Dr William R. Turner (the base leader/medical officer) and his team of dogs: Pundit, Millie, Ace, Scroop, Digger, Flash, Spud, Chopper and Ginny.

Shockingly, the Larsen A ice shelf no longer exists, having dramatically crumbled into the sea in 1995, due to global warming.

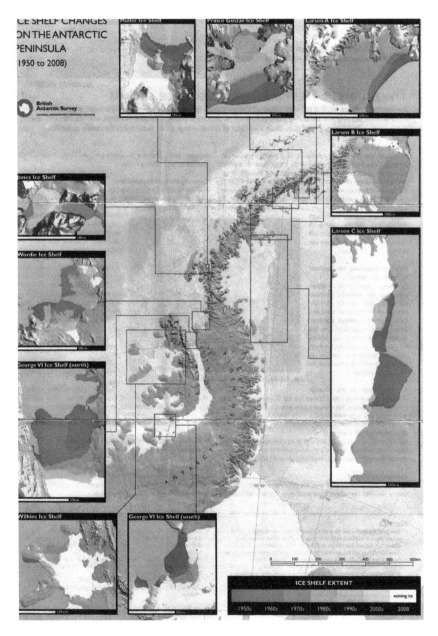

It had always been at the back of my mind, so when I saw the poster, I imagined myself in such a pose, and the fact that it was for a charity was even better. The charity was personal choice provided that the trip expenses were covered, all monies raised over and above that went to the charity.

I chose the Blue Cross animal charity which I felt was appropriate given the origin of the idea. 'The Blue Cross was founded in1897, originally to look after working horses in London, then later expanded in WW1 and WW2, and to cover other animals and geographical areas. The services now include veterinary facilities, rehoming of unwanted pets, bereavement support and welfare education.'

This then was my project for 2008. The challenge was to be in several parts: the fundraising, the expedition itself and the dogs (I am very much a cat person). Still, as someone once said to me "Feel the fear and do it anyway".

Some research was done using various sources including Wikipedia, various Arctic region sites, Norway Tourist Board, Villmarkssenter information sheets, Antarctic Survey Society, my own reminiscences, and discussions with other members of the challenge.

My thanks, firstly to Collette for her company and for looking after me in the cold Arctic countryside. To Simon and Penny for their support, physically, emotionally and financially. To Paula for looking after my cats and my house. To Mum, sisters Christine and Jean and to many friends for their support and donations. Also, to a number of strangers for their financial support. To Linda P. for the delicious food on the 'Moroccan Night', and Janice for her belly dancing exhibition. To Lez for technical discussions, to the publishers for proofreading services, and to 'Photo Corner', Bebington, Wirral for printing all of my photographs.

Many thanks to head guide and centre owner Tove Sorensen. To the other guides Tore Albrightsen, Mike Turner and Rene. Also, to Tomas and the staff at the Villmarkssenter Tromso, Norway.

And to my amazing husky team of Asterix, Santana, Masi, Yentna and Hel, for making a truly amazing time, even more incredible.

To David Bixter for the cover artwork.

And to Tamsin, Becky and all staff from Grosvenor House Publishing Ltd. for their help, advice, support and encouragement.

Introduction

> " In the icy air of night,
> Where the stars that over sprinkle
> All the heavens seem to twinkle
> With crystalline delight"
> From *The Bells* by Edgar Allan Poe

Planning

The information pack arrived with a proposed date of April 2008. The idea was to spend seven days in the company of a husky team, in the far north of Norway.

A very new experience having never done anything like it before, so, a first. There is something about 'firsts', that is so exciting, having an experience for the very first time and being aware of how special that time is going to be.

Collette and I got together to make a plan of action. There were several areas that we needed to sort out. The major ones: the funding, leave from our respective jobs, a fitness programme (especially in my case) and a gathering together of all of the required kit. This was April 2007, so we had a year to set everything in place.

Our leave duly booked, it was time to work on the other aspects.

Fundraising

We had both agreed that we would fully fund the 'expedition' part of the trip, it was not for other people to pay for our 'holiday' – although holiday was absolutely the wrong word for it. It was very hard work, and as the blurb had suggested it was certainly a challenge, but interesting and exciting for all that.

That paid for, we went about raising as much money as we could for our chosen charity. (Collette also chose the Blue Cross.) We organised some joint ventures involving our mutual friends, and some individual projects.

On the together front we organised a 'Race Night', such good fun where people were able to share in nominal amounts of winnings (so as to get the feel of a proper race meet), but where the bulk of the takings went to the charity, half from each of us. Food, drink, noise and laughter, a really successful, fun night. Everyone was very generous, so thank you all.

Our goal was to try to raise £3000 each, and we were now well on our way.

One of the local supermarkets gave us permission to do bag packing, a very busy day, but again people were very generous both in their donations and good wishes.

We had a themed night at my home, where for a small 'fee' invited guests were treated to a 'Moroccan style' night complete with specialist, and I must say, delicious food by Linda P. We were given a belly dancing exhibition by Janice – followed with great fun as the rest of us tried to learn some moves. I must say some of the men were pretty good at it too. Model-camel making and a prize for the most inventive name. A great night and again people were very generous.

A number of individual events took place such as sponsored bike rides, walking trips, question and answer sessions at our respective workplaces. In every case, people donated very generously. We hit our targets with no problem. So, a great big thank you to everyone.

Fitness Programme

Collette had always been fit, running, bike riding, swimming etc., but my case was completely different. What my mind could do, and what my body could do, were two entirely different things. Determination and enthusiasm could only take you so far.

Of course, when I was Collette's age I was much fitter and enjoyed playing things like netball and squash, but that had long been overtaken by, I would like to say other hobbies, what was in reality, just laziness. Only one answer, join a gym to increase my fitness levels, stamina, leg muscles and upper body strength. Much needed, I later found, when clinging onto a fast-moving sled being pulled along by five very enthusiastic huskies.

I altered my diet and my main achievement was to give up smoking – which was something I had done for many years. Please don't get me wrong, I did not suddenly become fit like Collette, but I was certainly better than when I started. Going to the gym was never my 'thing', so let's just say, I had a good go.

Kit Gathering

I had some kit from when I had gone trekking in the Annapurna region of Nepal (but that is another story).

However, I still needed snow wear, especially as the temperature could drop to -30 at night. Thermal underwear was an absolute must. Merino wool was the best type, not least because you could wear it for seven days before it started to smell. Also required were thermal socks, gloves, insulated, heavy-duty waterproof coat with hood, thermal trousers, good comfortable boots, hat, face-cover scarf. It was not advisable to have any bare skin open to the elements. Specially adapted sunglasses or snow goggles to complete the look.

An absolute essential was a warm sleeping bag, as near to polar or military grade as possible, and an under-bed roll. Sleeping in a tent can be cold at the best of times, and in those temperatures, well you can imagine.

Smaller items could be gathered later, such as cameras and batteries, water bottle, thermal mug with lid, energy bars and sweets, prescription pills as required, whistle, compass, head torch. A fuller kit list is in the appendix.

Journey

The leaving day came. Last minute checks, nervous phone calls with Collette, a meal with my family, hugs and kisses then a lift to the station for the overnight train to London and then Heathrow.

We arrived just before dawn. Inside the terminal we met up with the other people taking part in the trip. There were to be fourteen of us, from all over the UK.

Adventurers all.

It was fascinating meeting everyone, men and women, of different age groups, and soon we were being marshalled into place by our English guide, Mike.

Even though we were tired after our overnight journey, our excitement levels soon rose, and the tiredness disappeared.

Our first leg was a flight to Oslo where after a short layover, we were transferred to an internal flight up to Tromso.

Good flights, lots of chatter, interesting terrain to view and before long the seatbelt sign went on to prepare for the landing. Once through the checks and luggage retrieval, it was out into the arrival hall to be met by Tomas from the Villmarkssenter, We were treated to a thirty-minute trip through beautiful snow-coated hills and into the centre.

What amazing sights and sounds were to await us there.

Norway and the Arctic Region

A little background information:-
The Kingdom of Norway lies within the Scandinavian peninsula. It also includes the islands of Jan Mayen and Svalbard. Some areas are within the Arctic Circle.

It has a long coastline bordering the North Atlantic Ocean and the Barents Sea. It also has land borders with Sweden, Finland and Russia. Covering an area of over 324,000 square miles, with a current population of five million plus.
Capital city Oslo.

Thought to have been inhabited in coastal regions from 10,000 BC, rock carvings have been found outside Alta.
Also, Roman artefacts and runic inscriptions from 3AD. Settlements can be dated from their names.
From the ninth century, 'Things' became established. These were the regional assemblies and eventual seats of government of the various regions.

Norwegian Vikings were prolific during the 8th, 9th and 10th centuries founding settlements in England, Ireland and far-away places such as Newfoundland in Canada. Also in Iceland and Greenland. Throughout medieval times trade increased, and Norway became part of the Kalmar Union, a collective including Sweden and Denmark.

Norway suffered great population and financial losses due to failed harvests, and also to the Black Death that ravaged most of Europe, leading to the eventual forced union with

Sweden. This remained in place until 1905, when after a peaceful separation, the monarchy was reinstated in Norway.

Involved in both World Wars, large resistance movements were mounted in defence of their homeland.

Famous persons include the composer Grieg, artist Munch, playwright Ibsen and numerous sportsmen and women including Sonja Henie, Ole Einar Bjorndalen and Petter Solberg.

The major industries consist of oil, natural gas, fishing, farming, forestry, shipping, technology and paper production. The oil was discovered off the coast, thus allowing the growth of the country to what it is today. All proceeds being re-invested wisely'.

The scenery is known throughout the world to be of spectacular beauty, with its mountains, islands and fjords, and is a popular tourist destination both in summer and winter. The north of the country, in particular, experiences the Midnight Sun and the polar night.

The Northern Lights is an amazing sight, that remains with you for a lifetime. The phenomenon is caused when solar particles ejected from the sun meet the magnetic shield around the Earth and subsequently react with the atmosphere. The resulting dance of colours is magnificent.

The Arctic Circle is located at latitude 66° 33'N, roughly covers 9,900 miles and takes in parts of Canada, USA (Alaska), Russia, Finland, Sweden, Norway, Iceland and Greenland.

Defined by the northernmost point where the noon sun becomes invisible on the December solstice (Polar Night) and is visible all day at the June solstice (Midnight Sun).

The North Pole is about 1,650 miles from the latitude line of the Arctic Circle.

In the far north, temperatures can reach lows of -30°C, but it is warmer in the middle, inhabited regions. This is caused by various factors such as sunlight, heat, clouds and humidity. Norway is warmed by the Gulf Stream.

The first Arctic explorers were the Vikings, Norwegians, Icelanders and many countries since. The primary residents are now Inuit peoples, Sami and Russians.

(Information taken from Wikipedia, various Arctic Circle sites, World Atlas, Norwegian Tourist Board and my own knowledge.)

'SNOW DOGS'

Known as huskies they are thought to have come from the north-eastern regions of Asia.

The name husky is thought to have originated from words referring to Arctic peoples and to the dogs kept by the Inuit tribes.

There are various breeds, believed to share genetic markers with the now extinct Taimyr Wolf. They have a thick double coat in various colours such as black, white, grey and copper. They are often blue-eyed but can have other colours.

They are happy to be around people, very vocal, howling rather than barking, they are athletic, agile and intelligent.

Their breeds include:
The Siberian Husky – bred originally by the Chukchi peoples. They are medium sized working dogs, often characterised by their grey/white face masks.

Greenland Dog, a large powerful dog originally bred to hunt polar bears and seals, as well as for sled-pulling.

Alaskan Malamute, bred for hauling heavier loads, originally bred it is thought, by the Malamuit Inupiaq peoples from the Norton Sound area.

Alaskan Husky. Not a pure breed but a mix of the various northern breeds. Known for their speed and endurance, they are the ideal choice for racing. They are of moderate size, good with people and other dogs. Their colours and markings vary.

There are also some related breeds such as the Akita Inu and the Sakhalin (Japanese Sled Dog).

The dogs are used in various capacities.
Essentially, they are working dogs used for transportation of people and goods. They carry supplies, the mail and other requirements where there is no road system available.

They have taken part in rescue operations.

They have been used in Polar expeditions, most notably the Amundsen Expedition of 1911.

They are used in leisure activities such as Sled Dog Racing, Skijoring (pulling the owner along on skis), Carting (dry land mushing) and in endurance races such as the Iditarod.

They are also kept as pets. (Owners need to be aware of their specialised needs.)

The Iditarod was first run in March 1973 and covers 1000 miles from Anchorage to Nome in Alaska. The route includes dense forests, frozen rivers, mountain ranges and windswept coastal areas, mostly in temperatures below zero.

It was organised by Joe Redington Snr., to preserve the historical Iditarod trail (from Seward to Nome) and to save the sled dog culture. It can take between 10 and 15 days, an epic test of musher and dog fitness, stamina and mental fortitude.

Our two Norwegian guides Tove S. and Tore A. took part in the race in 2006.

The Iditarod was, in part, based on a true occurrence, known as the Nome Incident 1925, when there was a diphtheria outbreak in town and supplies of vaccine ran out. There was, however, some at nearby Nenana (nearby in Alaskan terms, 674 miles over virtually impassable terrain).

A dog sled relay was set up and twenty teams worked together to bring the serum to Nome.

Leonhard Seppala and his team with lead dog Togo, covered over 200 miles in atrocious weather (having first left Nome for Shaktoolik to pick up the serum from the previous musher), then returning to within 55 miles of Nome.

The last leg was covered by Gunnar Kaasen and his lead dog Balto. The serum was delivered, and the town saved from the ravages of the disease.

Both dogs were subsequently honoured for their part in the rescue, and all teams and their mushers passed into legend.

Part of the Iditarod circuit covers the original Nome route, in recognition of the heroic deeds carried out by the teams on the 'Serum' run.

TREK INFORMATION

Husky Trail Charity Challenge

Route
Birkenhead to London, UK
London – Oslo – Tromso, Norway Villmarkssenter Kvaloya
Island
Tromso – Oslo – London – Birkenhead, UK

Villmarkssenter
'An outdoors adventure centre.
Based on Kvaloya (the Whale Island). Owned by Tove
Sorensen, it is a family run business, aided by a multinational staff base.'

Trek Route

Norway
Galgojarvi
Golda
Gappo
Rosta
Mosko

Sweden
Paltsa
Store Rosta
Vosko
Salmi
Jukkasjarvi

Return to Tromso

Team Members

Guides:
Tove S.
Tore A.
Rene H.
Mike T.

Tomas, Liv and other Villmarkssenter staff

Team
Collette
Nina
Denise
Rosemary
Linda
Richard
Jools
Amanda
Gemma
Tracy
Jeff
Nicky
Bethany

Dogs
Asterix, Santana, Masi, Yentna and Hel
And over 240 other Alaskan-type Huskies.

Chapter One

Night in a Lavvo tent

We began with a taxi ride to Lime Street Station, the start of our journey into areas and experiences new.

We travelled on the overnight Liverpool–London train, negotiated the various changes on the underground system, finally reaching our destination of Heathrow. Still pre-dawn, we watched as the first fingers of morning lit up the sky.

At the meeting point, other members of the party had already gathered, having come from various parts of the UK. Fourteen intrepid travellers, including our guide, Mike.

Even though we were tired, our excitement levels soared seeing the others with their similarly large rucksacks, bedrolls and boots hanging from the straps. Quick introductions, then time to check in for our first staging flight to Oslo, followed by a final leg up to Tromso.

A good comfortable flight, a short layover at Oslo, then a smaller internal flight to our destination. The terrain had dramatically changed on the last section as we could see from the snowy vista viewed from the windows. White everywhere, broken by small dark areas which we could see were villages as they came into focus.

We touched down and were met by a minibus, to be taken to the Villmarkssenter where our adventure in earnest, was to begin.

A short drive across an elegant bridge took us from the main island of Tromso to the centre located on Kvaloya island, where a warm welcome and warm drink was awaiting us.

After the hellos, we were shown around the complex and then out to the compound. Well, what a sight, there must have been at least 250 dogs, of all sizes and colours. They were so pleased to see us, lots of friendly noises and tail wagging. Each had their own kennel with their names proudly displayed.

Names such as Ulrika, Gulis and even an Elvis. I am not a dog person (indeed that was part of the challenge for me), however, I was straight away smitten by how amazing and lovable these dogs were, and yet, in a moment, they immediately transformed into 'work mode', very businesslike, efficient and ready to go. I was very impressed and have loved huskies ever since.

We were also taken to the nursery section where there were a number of puppies being watched over by their vigilant parents, mother nursing and father guarding his little empire. We were told not to get too close, as with all parents the adult dogs were very defensive of their offspring.

After the tour, it was into the main building for a formal welcoming speech and food. A hot meal of reindeer stew, it was delicious, very filling and just what was needed after our travels.

Once fed, more introductions as we met the rest of the centre staff. Some were permanent, and others were previous trek members who had volunteered their services, like our guide Mike.

Next, we were given a series of talks on the natures of the dogs and how to treat them. They were working dogs and from the way we were greeted, very proud of it too. We were shown the technique of correctly attaching the harnesses.

This involved getting each of the dog's legs into the right section and ensuring that the 'body' section lay neat and comfortable along the spine of the dog. Also, to ensure it was the correct way up for the sled lines.

That may seem unnecessary to say but fumbling about in the half-light on the trail, when you are tired and cold, made it important to remember; and the dogs only had so much patience. Getting four excitable paws into a harness was a real challenge. They were not aggressive, they just wanted to get on with their jobs.

Our sleeping quarters for the night was a large communal tent, a Lavvo.

(After that it was to be individual two-person tents.)

We sat around a large log fire, learning more about the centre, the dogs and each other. Some of the team were friends like Collette and me, some were couples, some siblings and some lone members.

As the chatter died down, we set up our sleeping bags in a circle around the central fire, gradually one by one falling asleep.

Unfortunately, I was up in the night but was able to slip quietly out to the facilities a short walk away.

What a sight greeted me, the moon shone brightly overhead, lighting up the snow so that it glistened, like a diamond-studded path all the way to the loo. Silence. I was worried that I would disturb the dogs whose kennels I could plainly see, but luckily all stayed quiet.

I snuggled back into my sleeping bag and was soon asleep again.

We had an early morning start, washed, dressed and breakfasted. A last-minute pep-talk, then suddenly the whole place was an absolute bustle of activity.

Well, this was it, too late to have any second thoughts, this was where my *"Oh, that looks interesting..."* had brought me to; now it was to be a test of everything I knew, my stamina, my attitude, mental fortitude and physical strength.

Oh my, what had I done?

Chapter Two

Meeting the Dog Team

Over breakfast, we were reminded of our responsibilities to the dogs, to each other, to the equipment and the countryside.

We received the names of the dogs, who were to be our teams for the next week. Once ready we were taken out to meet our canine companions. They were Alaskan Huskies. My team comprised of Asterix, Santana, Masi, Yentna and Hel. (More about them later.)

We set off around the compound to find them. By this time the dogs knew was something happening, so there was much excitement around the centre. There were dogs everywhere, on their kennels or tethered beside them.

Bouncing up and down and so noisy, and yet friendly with much tail wagging as we approached. We had to keep in mind that these were working dogs, however that did not preclude their enjoyment of being stroked.

The guides would later load the dogs into the travelling kennels, for the drive out to the start point.

We were shown the sleds that would be carrying all of our equipment, the tent, food, personal belongings. They looked quite bulky and I thought about the dogs having to haul all of that weight and me on the end of it. I am not exactly a lightweight, if I am honest.

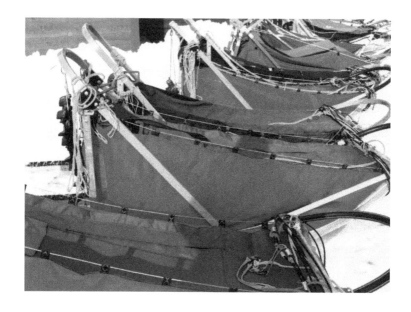

While we got our gear together, the guides started to ready the dogs. They had to be very careful that none got loose, or they would run off for hours. The general noise and activity around the camp rose to fever pitch.

The dogs were bouncing up and down and I am sure that if they could have talked, they would have said, "Take me, take me." The disappointment of the ones being left behind was very evident. We saw a team patiently waiting to take some cruise ship visitors on a ride. They were sitting so calmly amongst the general clamour.

What amazing creatures, my respect for them multiplied ten-fold.

Once the loading of the dogs was completed, the sleds were affixed to the roofs of the trailers, and all other equipment installed. We had not appreciated just how much was needed.

A last trip to you know where, then it was time for us to be loaded too. So, this was it, great excitement tinged with apprehension of what was awaiting us.

Too late now, we were off.

Our drive took us through some very striking countryside, across the bridges, past snow-laden hills until we reached our starting point, Helligskogen in the mountains, and the plateau at Golgojarvi. Once there a frenzy of activity unfolded before us.

The dogs remained in the kennels until the last moment. Prior to that, the sleds needed to be made ready and the food and equipment stowed away.

Each pair of people would be sharing a tent, so in our case, Collette and I had the stores distributed between our two sleds. This was to offload some of the weight that each team would have to pull.

Once loaded, the sleds were to be laid out in their travelling positions, the equivalent of F1 cars with Tove in pole position. Two guides at the front, one in the middle and the other at the end. Our sled train was set to be equipped with our requirements for the next week.

Collette had the tent and cooking equipment, I had all of the food containers. We each had our own personal packs. Quite a load for our dogs.

Once the harnesses and leads had been laid out, it was time to get the teams ready. This was done as quickly as was possible, as the dogs were very excited and eager to set off.

A last-minute pep-talk, reiteration of instructions and a practical demonstration of how the brakes worked. (The one on the sled and the independent claw anchor.)

All lined up and ready to go.

So, this was it, great excitement with a huge helping of 'OH, WHAT HAVE I LET MYSELF IN FOR THIS TIME?'

Too late, don't panic!

Chapter Three

Footing, Falls and Flying

One of the instructions that had firmly been drilled into us was, that if you fell, slipped or in any way lost your footing – do not let go of the sled.

That was to be sorely tested on at least four occasions the first day. It was not as if you could predict it, happily travelling along, then within seconds with your face in the snow, being dragged behind a runaway husky team.

Needless to say, even after much shouting of the STOP word, you would be left sitting in a snow bank, wondering what happened, watching your sled and dogs disappear over the horizon.

Fortunately, one of the reasons that the guides were up at the front was to stop such escapes. I was not the only one, it happened, on occasion, to most of the team, although we all improved greatly as the days went by.

The embarrassment of losing your dog team was coupled with the difficulty of, first, standing back up in the very deep snow, then the long trudge to where the runaways had been captured.

But, do not let me put you off, the exhilaration of the wind flying past your head, as you glided through the snow at unexpected speeds, was without compare. It was amazing.

Our cavalcade of sleds slid through the countryside, an impressive sight as we followed the trail laid down by the lead guides. Sadly, I had not mastered the technique of taking photographs on the move, but that would come later as my confidence grew. However, I used all rest periods to best effect.

We travelled through areas of the stunning Ovre Dividal Nasjonalpark.

The scenery was beautiful with forests of snow-laden trees, the silence punctuated only by the sound of the sled runners as they moved over the soft snow, and the occasional frantic, "Stoppe, stoppe, stop, STOP..." shouts from the various team members.

We halted for short breaks, mainly for drinks and energy bars until we came to our chosen campsite for the night. None of the breaks were for very long, as the dogs became restless and there was a danger that the lines would become tangled.

Our first night was spent in a forest area, close to a main trail, which had to remain clear for other 'traffic'. We had travelled over 30km.

There were a number of chores to be done that constituted 'making camp'. The first was to see to the dogs. A holding chain was attached between the trees then each dog in turn removed from the sled lines and attached with a shorter lead to the chain.

Food was collected and the team fed. It was fascinating to watch them make nests in the snow where, once settled, they stayed quietly for the night.

Collette saw to the feeding of our teams, while I was tasked with stamping down the snow to make a flat floor for the tent. The flatter the floor, the better the sleep.

After an abortive attempt, we got our tent up, our food stores installed inside, and of course, our bed rolls and sleeping bags. As with everything else, we got quicker as the days went by.

Our cooking equipment consisted of a number of pans interlocked like a stack of Russian dolls, quite ingenious.

The bottom sections became the little stove and the others, the cooking utensils.

The evening meals consisted of 'boil in the bag' stews so all we needed to find was the water.

Snow provided our water needs, which took some time to melt down. But before too long, wholesome food smells were coming from each tent.

A word of caution. You had to be very particular in your choice of snow, nothing with the slightest tinge of any colour, especially yellow, could be used.

The food made, more snow boiled up for the drinks, then it was time to refill the water bottles for the next day. We did not need to worry about cooling things down, we were living in a ready-made fridge. We ate our meal and got ready for sleeping. Just one more task, the little matter of the toilet. Now there was an interesting prospect.

We had brought with us, an 'aid' in the form of a plasticised funnel. Once inserted through the clothing, it could be used much in the style of a male appendage for passing urine. A little practice had been needed and it was very important to lean forward. It was not advisable to bare any flesh, especially in the up to -30°C temperatures at night. Anything else required a shovel and a well-chosen area. We all managed pretty well, thank goodness.

Once all of our chores were done, Collette and I sat with the tent flap slightly open and stared at the scene outside. The camp was quiet, just faint murmurings from the dogs, occasional voices on the air, the trees, the snow, the moon and stars. The whole scene ably summed up by E.A. Poe as in my opening quote from his poem *The Bells*. Everything 'twinkled', even the fur of the dogs as they lay in their snowy beds.

We slept well, all things taken into consideration. The bed rolls were perfect for keeping us off the cold floor of the tent, and the sleeping bags were just right for the job. I woke in the night, too hot, and shed some of my clothes layers down to my thermal underwear. I found sleeping like that was much more comfortable and continued to do so for the rest of the trip. Collette, however, was unconvinced and I think she wore more at night than in the daytime.

Breakfast consisted of high energy foods such as porridge and energy bars. The food boxes provided were very good and covered all of our needs. As the camp woke up, the dogs became restless wanting to move on. This was their job, after all, and they were very excited about being on the trail.

The sleds were repacked, and a clean-up operation put into place, which included the picking up and burying of any dog droppings. The whole area needed to be returned to the state in which it had been found when we arrived.

Time to move on through Isdalen, an ice valley of spectacular beauty. A journey to be of 60km.

Chapter Four

Talks in the Tent

The last thing to do, when breaking camp, was to re-attach the dogs to the sled.

We had been shown how to put on the harnesses, ready to clip back on to the main sled lines. I had fun with my big dog Asterix. The harnesses had to be put on in a certain way, forming a criss-cross pattern across the dog's back, each leg having a specific space. This was to evenly distribute the amount of pressure on the dog's body while pulling the sled. Their health, safety and comfort were of the utmost importance and under no circumstance should they be injured in any way.

So, back to Asterix, I had trouble getting his front leg into the harness. As I knelt beside him, on my third go, I caught sight of the expression on his face. As he very patiently held up his paw, his look of resignation very definitely said, *"I suppose I will have to help this amateur, or we will never get away. Where do they get them from...?"*

I was grateful.

After that, I managed the other dogs quite easily.

Before long, we were off, watching the forest slip by us as we followed the trail out to the open areas. Not so many falls this day, I was getting the idea. Just one major incident. I came off on a bend and managed to roll clear as two other sleds thundered by. The dogs travel very quickly and even though the stop commands were given, they took time to be implemented. The Norwegian trail version of a motorway incident.

As previously stated, I wasn't the only one who fell off, but the incidences decreased each day. How did we come to fall off? Well, there were a number of reasons. The runners where the 'driver' stood were very narrow, three inches at most, and most of the time covered in snow. It was easy to miss your footing after stepping off to help push the sled up the hills.

Once the hill was crested the dogs took off, so if you were too slow, you would be left with your nose in the snow being pulled along, or worse, watching your team disappear from sight. Fortunately, our choice of clothing protected us from injury. Another reason may be loss of balance when shifting your weight from side to side to take the corners, or just plain lack of concentration.

I did get better.

Later after a midday break for us all, especially the dogs, we moved through less forested areas and on to our night stop area, sledding on another 50km.

The routine was the same each time, firstly settle and feed the dogs, create a level area for the tent, cook the food and catch up on the day's events.

It was good to have our 'talks in the tent', recounting our experiences of the day, what we had seen, and how our points of interest differed. We managed to take some photographs, but mainly our talk was about our amazing dog teams.

Collette's dogs were black and white and looked rather like her two Border Collies at home, so she had an instant rapport with them. My bonding took a little longer, as I said, the dogs were part of the challenge for me, having only ever had one dog, and that was thirty years earlier.

We had a laugh but most nights we were so tired that we fell asleep pretty quickly. It amazed me that once settled and snuggled into their snow 'nests', there was no loud noise or movement from the dogs. Just gentle sighs as they shifted their positions during the night.

Sometimes, in the early hours, I would wake and just peek out at the scene outside. The whole camp would be just visible in the darkness, and I could make out the outlines of the tents, and the hazy shapes of the different dog teams asleep in the snow.

Quite magical.

P.S. One thing I learnt very quickly, was that if you wanted your camera to work, you had to keep it, and the batteries, warm overnight. Consequently, it shared my sleeping bag each night.

Chapter Five

Border Post

We had an earlier start, having now settled into the 'breaking camp' routine. We were all much more efficient at getting everything done. I had even mastered the harnesses, thanks to the help of Asterix. He was not the lead dog, but he was my number one dog, I had developed a real fondness for him.

The actual two lead dogs were Yentna and Hel. They worked in tandem at the front of the lines and were the clever ones who listened to and obeyed the commands. It was they who stopped and started the sled. I had thought that they just followed the other teams, but on one occasion I had to shout directional commands, gee and haw, which they followed, even allowing for my strange accent. (See glossary.)

The first command that we all learnt was stoppe (stop) to which the dogs responded admirably. It took quite some doing to stop a team running at full pelt with a heavy sled, and heavy person, behind them. This was normally only if someone had fallen up ahead, to avoid a collision. The dogs did it well. I had so much respect for them.

Masi was the middle runner, sweet-natured and quite the athlete, and then came the two big boys Asterix and Santana. They were nearest to the sled and were the powerhouse of the team. Each dog had his/her own function within the team, and they all absolutely earned their rest at the end of the day.

Their toiletry needs were mainly attended to on the run, they truly were amazing animals.

The terrain changed as we started to leave the forested areas behind and moved out on to an open plain.

The snow was much deeper and therefore more difficult for the dogs. Where we could we would get off the runners and help to push the sled.

After a while, the land and the sky started to blur into one, known as a 'white-out', so we were very thankful for the red-crossed marker poles which showed the best track.

We weren't overly worried because we knew that the lead guides Tove and Tore carried GPS equipment on their much larger sleds, ably pulled along by their teams of ten dogs.

We stopped for a rest and photographic session on the plateau. The snow sparkled even though there was no obvious sun. If anyone else had passed that way, it was not evident, as the only tracks were ours. We began a slow climb up a long gentle incline. Near the top, we stopped again. It was quite a view looking back, seeing all of the other teams snaking up the hill.

At the top of the ridge were several wooden huts, which we were told was the Border Post and administrative buildings between Norway and Sweden.

We rested while our guides presented our paperwork for inspection. It seemed to be more of a courtesy call as there were no posts or fences. However, that did not mean there was no security, there were a number of personnel.

While these checks were being carried out, we took the opportunity to drink our water and have our energy bars and snacks. The dogs, I am sure, were the most happy with the rest, they had worked very hard getting us to that point and we could see them snuggling down in the snow.

I, by this time, had begun to feel the effects of the trek and my stamina levels had begun to drop, slowly at first then quite dramatically. I knew that I was older than the others, but I had done a certain amount of training, so I was surprised. Riding the sled was the easier part, making and breaking camp became more difficult. (I found out later that there was a medical reason for this.)

All checks completed, we started on the next phase, which was to arrive at the 'Fish Camp'. This part proved to be the most difficult for me as it involved riding down the steeper side of the hill we had just climbed but with added obstacles such as trees, narrow trails and bridges. A real test of skill for all concerned.

The dogs were magnificent and deftly manoeuvred their way around the obstacles. My job was to ensure that the sled did the same. Changes in direction were achieved by shifting body weight from runner to runner and leaning in the direction of the turn. Applying of the brakes was only for emergencies and after instructions had been given to the dogs. No sudden jerking that might injure the team.

Collette's team was in front of mine, and I watched in awe as she hopped from runner to runner, striking poses, like that of a ballerina. Back arched and both feet on one runner, her glissade was 'poetry in motion'.

My efforts sadly were much more clumsy. I did not have the confidence, or the balance, to take my feet off the runners, but instead shifted my whole weight from one side or the other. A perfectly acceptable way of doing it, but it did not have the artistry of Collette.

The main difficulty with taking your feet away from the runners was finding them again. As said earlier, they were very narrow and when covered in snow, became very hard to see. Once an obstacle was cleared, the dogs were off in a great burst of speed, with the potential of leaving a very surprised you, sitting in the snow, watching them disappear from sight.

One last obstacle. A very steep downward hill with an almost 90-degree turn at the bottom, I must say that I found it very daunting. Luckily, once again the dogs really showed their mettle and it helped that Tore was at the bend ready to encourage those of faint heart (that would be me).

Once the ground had flattened out, it was a clear run to the 'Fish Camp'.

It was thrilling, breathtaking, invigorating, the wind rushing past, looking out at the amazing countryside where the only visible evidence of human occupation was the tracks of the teams in front of you. On the flat, the dogs could reach speeds of over 20mph.

We reached another plateau where a lone man, with his snowmobile and flat-bed trailer, awaited us. He was the custodian of the camp, come to meet us.

The camp was a welcome respite from sleeping out in the tents, an oasis of wooden huts on a snow-clad hill. Of course, the needs of the dogs were attended to first, as they were to remain on the plateau. Long tethering lines were firmly anchored to the ground and each team attached, much in the way that had been done at the overnight stops.

Two guides and some volunteers opted to stay with the dogs and set about erecting their tents.

The rest of us were taken to the camp, riding gratefully on the trailer.

Chapter Six

Fish Camp, Snowmobiles and a Reindeer Dog

The camp, a very welcome sight, was comprised of a number of wooden huts, including a civilised 'facilities' block.

We were to share with Rosemary and Nicky. My heart soared when the door opened, there were bunks, a table, chairs and in the middle a lit stove that provided both warmth and cooking facilities. No searching for untarnished snow, as water was available from a specifically dug hole in the ground, fresh and clean.

While the stew was cooking, we got our bunks ready. What luxury. We hung our sleeping bags to dry out as they had picked up condensation from inside the tents. Much of our clothing was also damp, so it was a wonderful opportunity to dry things off. The hut took on the appearance of a commercial-scale laundry.

The toilet block was still pretty primitive, cubicle seats over a cesspit, but there were no complaints from me, it was warmer and easier to use than all previous methods.

Warm and full, we all chatted about our experiences so far, our motivations for coming, our general lives and just normal chit-chat. As well as raising money for our various charities, it was in each case a trip of self-awareness, of how to face and deal with the many challenges, of attitudes, thoughts and dreams.

I had begun to feel unwell with a deep-rooted lethargy. Of course, everyone was tired, but it felt more than that. Collette began to worry about me and after a very honest conversation between the two of us, she went to see the guides. I was called to a meeting to discuss what to do next.

I was told that I could return, with the camp manager, to a specified point to await pick-up by Villmarkssenter staff. However, if I stayed after this there would be no point of return until the end of the trek. The most arduous part of the trek was still to come, down to the frozen lake at Jukkasjarvi, another 60km on.

After much discussion, and with a great deal of disappointment, I opted to go back. I was upset to be leaving Collette on her own to cope with the tent, the dogs, and the meals, after a hard day on the trail.

She, of course, was wonderful about the whole situation. (I found out when I got home that I had a condition that affected my heart rate and oxygen intake.) I had a good cry and slept fitfully.

The next morning, I spent time wishing everyone well. They were all very understanding, there were hugs all around, and a few tears. Actually, more than a few tears, especially when I thought of my wonderful dogs who were down on the plateau. They were to be distributed out amongst the other teams, I was sorry not to say goodbye to them, especially my stoic Asterix. The sled was to come with me.

The sled train moved on, leaving me to wave it sadly goodbye.

Time came for us to leave too, the manager, whom I shall call Nils, attached my sled to the back of his snowmobile. I climbed on to the back seat, and as we set off a large brown dog appeared and jumped on between us. It was his reindeer dog. At first, I held on to him (the dog) thinking that he would fall off, but after a while I realised that he was well used to it, gently swaying with the movement of the machine, his balance absolutely perfect. Unlike me, who was clinging on to anything I could hold.

Once I relaxed, the journey was amazing, at one point I saw a herd of reindeer in the distance. The dog was very firmly told to stay put, which he did, although he was allowed off later.

We travelled up and down hills, past streams, swaying around tree stumps, kicking up clouds of snow, it was incredible, what an experience.

We finally came to a small built-up area. The dog was fed and sent to be looked after by a friend. Preparations were made for the remainder of the trip. I was to be picked up at a truck stop in Finland, near the Norwegian border. At this juncture, we were still in Sweden.

There were several tarpaulined shapes, underneath one of which, was an old Saab covered in icicles.

This, I was informed was our transport. "We'll be lucky to get that going," I thought negatively. I thought about winters in England where everything stopped.

Nils gently blew on the door lock and inserted the key. With no resistance at all, it opened. The interior was very cold, but without hesitation, he placed the key in the ignition and turned it once. The car's engine sprang into life. My jaw dropped, he smiled and said, *"We will leave it ticking over for a few minutes to warm up, it hasn't been used for a month."* Well, that's Swedish technology for you, built to stand up to the harshest climates.

While I stood about being useless, he proceeded to load my sled on to the car's trailer. A quick comfort stop, and we were off.

Farewell Sweden.

Chapter Seven

Return to Tromso

The rendezvous point was at a large roadside cafe in Finland, in an area where the borders of the three countries (Sweden, Finland and Norway) met. Nils and I spent a pleasant hour chatting about families and life generally, as we travelled through forested regions, past the occasional village until we reached the intersection and the location of the cafe. Once my sled was off-loaded, we said our goodbyes.

I spent the next hour eating lunch and looking out of the window, as the Scandinavian world passed by, waiting for Tomas and Liv to come from the Villmarkssenter. My sled was parked on a snow-covered verge.

It looked so forlorn, rather how I felt.

I had a few quiet tears, disappointed to have come back, but I knew it was the right decision.

I thought of the others going on to the Ice Hotel, with more than a tinge of jealousy, but unbeknownst to me at that point, I would get my chance to go there, albeit six years later.

The Norwegian rescue crew arrived, loaded the sled onto the roof of the vehicle and me into the back seat. My muscles by now had gone into 'screaming' mode, my adrenaline levels dropped to rock bottom and an intense tiredness hit me. I fell asleep immediately.

I awoke to witness the most amazing scenery, snow-covered mountains, one of which was called "the sleeping soldier". The vehicle was stopped, and I was helped out to take some photographs.

The dazzling whiteness of the snow against the very blue sky was stunning. The air was clear, you could just taste the purity of it, the whole scene was truly awe-inspiring. I stood, overwhelmed by the sight of it all. There is just something so magical about that kind of scenery.

Tomas particularly was very supportive as I was very obviously upset at not completing the whole trek. He told me to be proud of my achievement as very few people, including Norwegians, had done what I had done. His words were comforting, so I relaxed and went back to sleep.

Another photographic opportunity was taken as we came back into Tromso, over the Tromsoysundet Strait.

On arrival back at the centre, I was warmly welcomed by the other staff with hugs and a hot drink. I was also given a puppy to hold, only weeks old. So cute, beautiful blue eyes, very alert. He gave me the impression that he already knew his role in life and was eager to get on with it.

I could not get over just how amazing these dogs were, my respect for them has lasted ever since.

I was taken to the hotel where we had been booked for the last night, now in my case, two nights. I stood in the shower for a long time letting the hot water play over every aching muscle. What bliss. Another rest, then food.

The hotel was situated on the bay and had a stunning view across the water to the mainland. As darkness fell, lights sparkled from the street lamps, the houses, the bridge and the outlines of the buildings on the other side of the Strait. The silence only broken by the soft buzz of half-heard conversations and occasional car noise.

What a place, added to which "All the heavens seemed to twinkle, with crystalline delight".

Beautiful. I had travelled to many places in my lifetime, but I had never felt such clearness and being part of the air as I did here. I absolutely loved it.

Back in my room, I thought over my feelings about everything, about my limitations, but also about my achievements, I did not want disappointment to spoil what was left of my time in this amazing place.

I decided that I would go sightseeing and take the opportunity, not afforded to the rest of the team, to see Tromso in its own right.

The plan thus made, I went to bed and had a good sleep.

I did not miss having to stamp down the snow to make a level sleeping area or putting up the tent. I did not miss the boiling of the snow for the drinks. But I did miss the gentle breathing of the dogs as they settled for the night, and the chats with Collette as we recounted our thoughts and feelings of the day's events.

The early morning sun woke me, another hot shower to get those muscles working, breakfast then out. This was to be my unique bit of the challenge, hitting the tourist trail.

Chapter Eight

Churches, Cable Cars
and Cold Callers

I walked up from the harbour to the shopping area. The city stretched over three distinct sections, the main one being Tromsoya island. I passed some modern hotels, municipal buildings and wooden houses.

I saw the Fisherman statue, sculpted by Sivert Donali in 1984, a homage to the whaling community, former industry of the area.

Although designated as a city, the whole place had a small-town feeling.

In the distance I saw a church, which I decided to visit and photograph, something I had done in many areas of the world. This was a Lutheran church and as such was simply and sparsely decorated.

Inside, I sat back quietly and got lost in my thoughts. My reverie was broken by a concerned woman asking if I was feeling well. We struck up a conversation and before long I was sitting with a cup of tea, and the vicar had been summoned from the vestry.

A little audience gathered, interested in my name, why I was there, my family background, and most importantly where I was staying.

My reason for being there, I was able to tell them in great detail, regaling them with stories from the trail. My background, as they could tell from my surname, was of Scandinavian ancestry, a great-grandfather from a place called Hallaryd near the southern coast of Sweden.

Where I was staying, well that was a little more tricky. I knew roughly where it was, but not its name. This appeared to cause some consternation and resulted in a second cup of tea. After a while, I assured them I was well and would go back to the hotel.

I wandered back and once back in my room, my mirror told me why they were so concerned. My face was very white apart from two bright red cheeks, that coupled with my slowness and unsteadiness of walking, they must have thought I had a raging fever.

However, all had logical explanations, the gait was due to muscle fatigue after having clung to the back of a sled for six days, the red cheeks compliments of windburn and the rest, just plain tiredness.

I actually felt well, but I was touched by their concern and it was heartening to know that my welfare was in their thoughts.

After lunch, I decided to again venture out. I checked the hotel address. It was to be a cultural afternoon with visits to museums. Armed with leaflets and a map, I was able to find the places with ease. I walked through a small park, breathing in the fresh clear air.

The life of the explorer Roald Amundsen was depicted in the Polar Museum, with many fascinating artefacts and photographs from Polar expeditions, including his epic race with Scott (December 1911). Amundsen reached the South Pole thirty-four days ahead of Scott.

How different was the approach of the two men, one using dog teams, the other ponies and manpower. Both parties very brave, but sadly Scott and his team perished, to become part of England's rich history.

The Natural History Museum was a bus ride away, an efficient, clean, comfortable service as expected. This museum showed life how it had been and how it was now.

Examples of the Sami peoples, the whaling communities and the emergence of Norway as a nation. I have always enjoyed learning about the places I have visited.

'Sami peoples were the indigenous tribes of Lapland, an area that lay across Norway, Sweden, Finland and part of Russia. Traditionally they made their living from herding reindeer, livestock farming, fishing and hunting. In more recent times some people had settled in the towns and cities. Land right battles had been going on for many years, but finally in 2013, their rights were recognised.'

Back on the bus trail, this time to the Cable Car station and up to the top, from where the whole of Tromso, in all of its glory, could be seen.

I stood on the viewing platform and took many photographs. While there, I met Petter who had come up the mountain on skis, pulled by his two huskies. Both dogs were of the Siberian Husky type with their distinctive grey/white face masks.

Powerful beasts, a father and son, who waited patiently while Petter and I swapped stories, mainly about Liverpool. He was a huge football fan. I have learnt that no matter where in the world you go, there are always fans who will "Never walk alone".

After our goodbyes, a funny little incident occurred. My mobile phone rang.

"Hello, is that Nina?"

"Yes."

"This is your car insurance company calling, can I just take some details?"

"Well, actually, I do not have them to hand at the moment, I am up a mountain in Norway."

There was a pause, then a disbelieving, *"Yeah, right,"* and the receiver went down.

Oh. She must have thought she had heard every excuse there was, but in this case, it was true.

Funny thing about excuses, the more outrageous they are the more likely they are to be true. While a mature university student, I missed a whole day's classes. Very unlike me. The following day I was met by worried class mates and lecturers.

"Were you ill?"

"No."

"Overslept?"

"No, I'm afraid I don't have a very good excuse, but you see, I spent the day running around waving a red carnation, with a placard-bearing youth."

Silence.

The explanation was that I got involved with a film crew on my way to the college, and spent the day being an extra on a film that I thought, at first, my idol Gary Oldman was in (turned out to be Daniel Day-Lewis).

The silence lengthened, then everyone laughed. The lecturer said, *"Oh, I don't know, that is one of the best excuses I have ever heard."*

I suppose they did not expect that type of behaviour from a forty-something, mother of two, mature student. Expected or not, I had a great day.

I digress, back to my Tromso wanderings. I had a very scenic bus ride around the city, then back to my hotel.

Later, looking out of my window at the lights of the harbour and the mainland beyond, I thought of how lucky I was for this whole experience. I caught sight of the iceberg-shaped cathedral, aglow in the darkness.

Definitely a visit for the morrow.

Chapter Nine

Celebrations and Goodbyes

I felt much better after a good night's sleep, my muscles had stopped aching, so, fitter in mind and body, I planned my route to the cathedral.

The rest of the team were returning that afternoon, so I had decided to fill my morning with more sightseeing before it was time to get ready for the evening celebrations. I wanted to ensure that the shower was free for Collette, I know how grateful I was to wallow in the soothing waters.

The bus came and it struck me how different everything looked to the day before. The greyness had given everything a heavy feeling, all colours dulled and the snow a dirty tinge. This day, however, all was changed, the sun shone and lit up everywhere. The snow sparkled, and the houses looked as if they had been newly painted, the scene spread out like a quilt of many colours.

I chatted to a fellow bus traveller, originally from the USA but now domiciled in Tromso. I had met a number of local people, some of whom were from other countries but had made their homes in Norway, I could understand why. I found everyone to be helpful and friendly, making me feel part of the city, not just a visiting stranger.

After a little tour around the city, the bus reached the cathedral. An imposing edifice 'built 1964/1965, the vision of architect Jan Inge Hovig. In 1972 the Victor Sparre glass mosaic window had been installed. The magnificent window depicted Christ, of monumental design, 23 metres high and covered an area of 140 square metres. The cathedral was built mainly of concrete and was designed to represent an iceberg, as seen in the seas around the Arctic Circle.'

Sadly, I was not able to go in as there was a roof renovation being carried out. I was, as you can imagine, disappointed, but hoped that I would be able to return at some time in the future.

Later, I got a phone call from Collette to say that their return was imminent. I went to the foyer to meet them. Such excitement as the 4x4s pulled in and off-loaded their tired but happy occupants.

It was good to see everyone.

Back in the room, Collette did exactly as I had done on returning – enjoyed a hot, muscle-soothing shower.

A short relaxing sleep, then much chatter as she told me of her adventures once I had left. Sounded like hard work to me, although for someone fit like Collette it would have been fine.

Marshmallows around a fire, hot berry juice, the frozen lake and of course, the Ice Hotel. It sounded amazing. I, too, had had my adventures, but while they had fed their sense of adventure and excitement, I had fed my vision and mind.

Wearing the best clothes that we had with us, we emerged from our room ready for the evening festivities, to be held in a nearby restaurant.

After the meal we told 'tales from the trail', each from a very different perspective. Mine involved snowmobiles and reindeer dogs.

Time for the presentation of the certificates. Each person was given a medal and certificate marking their participation in the challenge. I wondered if I would qualify but was told that as I had completed the bulk of it I would also receive mine. So, with the approval of the rest of the team, I happily accepted.

Some music, lots of chatter and a happy walk back to the hotel completed the night. What an experience we had all had.

Too excited to sleep, but sleep we must, for tomorrow we would be going home.

Chapter Ten

Home

After the last night's festivities, we awoke ready to complete the final part of our trip.

Once breakfasted, we brought our luggage to the hotel reception ready for our last minibus ride to the airport. We would later say our goodbyes (via Tomas) to the Villmarkssenter, to Tove and the other guides, to the dogs and to Tromso.

We had a couple of hours to wander around the city, to buy mementos and presents to bring home. For myself, I bought a small husky toy, which still hangs in my car window, a constant reminder of the adventure of a lifetime.

Time to load onto the minibus.

I stared from the window at the stunning countryside as it rolled by, I could not believe that the time had gone so quickly and that we were actually on our way home. Eight days, but it felt like forever, we had seen and done so much.

I was very sorry to have missed the last part of the trek, but I was lucky enough to have had an adventure of my own and time to do some sightseeing. Initially, I felt that I had failed, but was heartened by the supportive words of Tomas who made me appreciate my achievement. As he said, there cannot be that many people who have been there and done that.

The views and reflections from the windows, the highs and lows, were echoed in my internal reflections. As with many of my other adventures, part of the experience is learning about yourself, your capabilities and limitations and learning to accept and overcome them.

Once the formalities had been addressed, it was on to the plane and time to relax. The flights were good and in what felt like very little time, we were touching down at Heathrow.

Hugs all around as we said goodbye to our fellow team members, each taking home, I am sure, some amazing memories.

On the journey back to Birkenhead, I must say I slept most of the way and awoke, happy to see my family at the pick-up point.

Fond farewells with Collette and plans made to meet up, reminisce and look at the photographs. I have always had my photographs developed as soon as possible and put into albums. (I have often sat with a cup of tea and thought "Where shall I go today?", reached for one of my albums and travelled off into my memories, to relive the whole experience.)

So here I was,
HOME, my Zen place.

Hello to my cats, to Paula who again had looked after everything for me, and later to Simon and Penny. Feet up, I just let my mind run wild. What an experience, I had never done anything like it in my entire life. I thoroughly enjoyed it, even though I had found it difficult, but after all, isn't that what challenges are all about?

What sights I had seen, with my oh so patient dog team. What a laugh with the other team members. What an amazing experience I have had and was lucky enough to share with a good friend like Collette.

Thank you, to all.

Later (October, same year).
Mike, our English guide invited Collette and I to a Husky Meet in Delamere forest – no snow, but 'sleds' with wheels and numerous teams of enthusiastic huskies. Great fun.

Much later, (six years later in fact).
I went, with various friends, on a rail trip from Birkenhead to Beijing (but that, of course, is another story).

I travelled up to Kiruna in Sweden, as part of the Scandinavian leg of the trip. While there, my friend Gill and I went on a short husky team excursion with guide Jan. Our destination was the very same frozen lake at Jukkasjarvi that I had missed in 2008. Finally, I was able to complete my Husky Charity Challenge, added to which Jan had worked at the Villmarkssenter in 2010, with two of my dog team.

"All things come to those who wait."

Nina xxx

POSTSCRIPT

Reminiscences of My Husky Adventure
250 Alaskan Huskies
Named Kennels
Puppies
Centre Guides
Snow
Travelling Kennels
Sleds
Food containers
Harnesses
Tents
Stars
Trails
Forests
White-out
Border Post
Trail markers
Rivers
Snowmobile
Reindeer dog
Car
Fish Camp
Mountain
Cable Car
Museums
Cold weather clothes
Other team members
Collette, Tove, Tore, Rene, Mike, Tomas, Nils
Asterix, Santana, Masi, Yentna and Hel

"Sled Train" by Mike Turner (Guide)

APPENDIX

1. Transport

Train

       Liverpool to London Heathrow

Plane

SAS   London – Oslo

SAS   Oslo – Tromso

SAS   Tromso – Oslo – London

Minibus

       Airport to Villmarkssenter Kvaloya Island

       Centre to Plateau

       Finland pick-up to Centre

Car   Sweden to pick-up point in Finland

Snowmobile

       'Fish Camp' Sweden to car location

Husky Team

       Villmarkssenter Norway to 'Fish Camp'
       Sweden

Accommodation

       Tent – various locations

       Hotel   Tromso

Miscellaneous

       Passport

       Travel Insurances

2.

Kit List (suggestions)
Waterproof Boots
Warm waterproof coat
Waterproof over trousers
Fleece
T-Shirts
Thermal underwear
Thermal socks
Thermal waterproof gloves (inners and outers)
Sleeping Bag (for temps. below -20°)
Roll-up mattress
Snow goggles
Large rucksack
Travel towel
Toiletries, Sun cream and Lip Salve
Toilet Roll
First Aid Pack
Prescription Medicines
Whistle and Compass
Notebook and Pen
Camera, Batteries, Cards, Films
Waterproof bag for pills, paperwork etc.
Eating utensils
Water bottle and Thermocup with lid
Energy bars/sweets
Smart(ish) outfit for Certificate Ceremony
Head Torch
Reading material if desired
Other kit as recommended

3.

Glossary
Gee – turn right (husky command)
God dag – good day
Haw – turn left (husky command)
Hike – get moving (husky command)
Hund – dog
Lavvo – Sami temporary dwelling
Mush – thought to come from 'marche' (French explorers)
Norwegian – north Germanic language
Oy – island
Sami – indigenous peoples of the Arctic region
Seletoy – harness
Sno – snow
Stoppe – stop
Takk – thanks
Telt – tent
Venn – friend
Villmarkssenter – Wilderness Centre
Voer se snill – please

Blue Cross
The Blue Cross was founded in 1897. It was originally set up to care for working horses in London, under the name of 'Our Dumb Friends League charity'. Much work was carried out during WW1 and WW2. The charity has since evolved to include other animals and provides various functions such as: Veterinary services, the rehoming of unwanted animals, pet bereavement support, and promotes welfare through education and knowledge.

INDEX